I0053691

kid$ense
Presents

The
Debt Monster

Mary Becker
Illustrations by Tim Williams

To my husband, our children, their spouses,
and our adorable grandchildren . . .
Each of you has brought me much joy
and happiness, more than any amount of
money could ever supply!

—Mary

BOOKLOGIX®
Alpharetta, GA

Although the author and publisher have made every effort to ensure that the information in this book was correct at the time of first publication, the author and publisher do not assume and hereby disclaim any liability to any party for any loss, damage, or disruption caused by errors or omissions, whether such errors or omissions result from negligence, accident, or any other cause.

Copyright © 2016 by Mary Becker

All rights reserved. No part of this book may be reproduced or transmitted in any form or by any means, electronic or mechanical, including photocopying, recording, or any information storage and retrieval system, without permission in writing from the publisher. For more information, address BookLogix, c/o Permissions Department, 1264 Old Alpharetta Rd., Alpharetta, GA 30005.

Second Edition

ISBN: 978-1-61005-762-2 - Paperback
ISBN: 978-1-6653-0545-7 - Hardcover
eISBN: 978-1-61005-763-9 - ePub
eISBN: 978-1-61005-764-6 - Mobi

Library of Congress Control Number: 2016902748

10 9 8 7 6 5 4 3   1 1 1 4 2 2

♾ This paper meets the requirements of ANSI/NISO Z39.48-1992 (Permanence of Paper)

Cover art and illustrations by Tim Williams

Introduction

FOR TEACHERS AND PARENTS

The message of *The Debt Monster* tells us to avoid the materialistic culture that surrounds us. Our "me-me-me" centered society emphasizes the concept that buying and showering a child with lots of things (no matter the price or debt-related cost) is the best way to give a child what (s)he wants to achieve happiness. In truth, what a child wants will not supply what the child really needs; (s)he needs you, your time, and your undivided attention. This story will help you teach children the difference between wants and needs, the importance of being patient in waiting until they can afford certain things, and the value of being content and thankful for what all of us have already . . . each other! Happy reading!

Remember! You can **S.T.A.N.D.** with others against the debt monster:

Spend

Time

And

Not

Dollars!

There once was a family who just loved to shop.
They loved it so much that they never could stop.
At least once a day they would go to a store.
It was never enough; they always bought more.

One day when they shopped, the cart was so filled,
When they tried to push it, everything spilled.

Clothes, toys, and a bike . . . and oh, so much more.
It went everywhere . . . everywhere . . . covering the floor.

They picked it all up and stacked it real high,
But that didn't stop them; they continued to buy.

Peanuts and popcorn and even some fish.
They bought anything (and everything!) . . .
   Whatever they wished.

Candy and goodies . . . even holey Swiss cheese.
And the last thing they chose was made by some bees.
On the top of the cart, they balanced the honey,
But when they got to the checkout,

They had run out of money!

"There's no cash in my purse, ATM, or the bank!"
The mom was embarrassed;
    The children's hearts sank.

"Don't worry," said Dad, "I'll just charge it with plastic.
This card is like money. You'll see it's fantastic!"

"Of course," said the mom, "just listen to Dad.
We can have all our wants and never be sad."

"Excuse me, dear folks," said the little old man.
"But I think it is best if you have a plan.
When you come to the store, you should know what to buy.
Write it all on a list; you should give this a try.
And know how much money that you have to spend
For that charge card you hold is not really your friend."

"You see," the clerk said, "the debt monster is scary.

"He's **LARGE** and he's GREEN, and he's really quite hairy.
He's standing right by you. He's ready and willing
To start eating your money; it's really quite chilling."

"Oh my," said the dad as he looked at the beast,
"I thought charging was harmless . . . risk-free at least."

"Excuse me, kind sir," said one child to the clerk,
"What is this thing debt and how does it work?"

"Debt usually is an invisible deal;
But now you can see that debt is so real.
This debt monster here is a really tough guy;
He makes you pay extra for stuff that you buy."

"He comes to live with you; he's there every day,
When you have no money but promise to pay.

And once he moves in, it is hard to be free;
All the bills must be paid for the monster to flee."

The monster was angry; he wanted to stay.
Being debt-free meant he would go away.
He opened his mouth and roared,
"Go ahead!
You can charge all these things;
You have nothing to dread!
Hurry up! Charge it now!" the monster did jeer.
"You can take all this home; you have nothing to fear!"

The children were silent. They looked at the stuff.
They had stuff at home; they did have enough.

"Oh please, Mom and Dad," said the girls and the boy.
"We don't need these things; not even a toy!
We want that debt monster to stay far away;
Let's not go into debt so you have more to pay!"

"We want that debt monster to *GET OUT OF HERE!*"
And when the monster heard that, he did disappear!
The mom and the dad, they looked at each other.
Then smiled at the children, the sisters and brother.
"Help us remember **NO CHARGING WITH PLASTIC!**
No debt monster near us means life is fantastic!"

So the family went home, left the stuff at the store,
And learned a great lesson:
   NOT TO CHARGE ANYMORE!

They now know the difference between a "want" and a "need,"
And they shop with a list to which they've agreed.
Now when they are looking for something to do
They don't go to a store . . . They try something new.

Like hiking or biking or drawing with chalk;
They play baseball or football or sometimes just talk.
They love being together WITHOUT all the stores.
They are happy (and spend less), plus enjoy living more!

Clerk Moe Frugal's

Ideas for Discussion

1. In the beginning of the story, when the mom didn't have cash to pay for the items they wanted to buy, the dad decided to charge the items with "the plastic" charge card. Did you know there is another kind of plastic card called a debit card? Discuss the difference between a charge card and a debit card. When should you use a debit card? Is there ever a time when you should use a charge card?

2. The I. O. Lots family bought whatever they wanted. Discuss the difference between a "want" and a "need." Can you think of some things that you need? What are some things that you want?

3. Moe Frugal said it was wise to have a plan before going to a store to shop. How do you make a shopping plan? What would you put on the list?

4. Debt is when you pay extra for stuff that you buy. How can you help keep the debt monster away?

5. At the end of the story, the family left the stuff they didn't need at the store. Can you think of a time when you did the same?

6. What are some fun things you and your family would like to do together instead of going to a store to shop for things that you really don't need?

7. And just for fun . . . How many debt monsters can you find in the book? Look carefully; the debt monster is very tricky!

Grade Level Dolch Sight Word List Found In
The Debt Monster

Pre-primer			
a	help	make	the
and	here	me	to
away	I	not	we
can	in	one	you
come	is	run	.
for	it	said	
go	little	see	

Primer			
all	into	please	well
at	like	so	went
be	must	that	what
but	no	there	who
did	now	they	with
get	on	this	
have	our	want	
he	out	was	

Grade One			
an	his	old	then
as	how	once	think
by	just	some	were
could	know	stop	when
give	live	take	
had	of	them	

Grade Two			
always	don't	right	work
best	green	these	would
buy	made	us	write
does	or	wish	your

Grade Two		
far	if	never
got	kind	start
hold	much	try

Glossary

ATM: a bank machine that lets you put money into a bank or take it out without going inside a bank. ATM means Automatic Teller Machine or Automated Teller Machine

bank: a business where people put their money

bills: a list telling the amount of money you owe for something you've bought

charge: to wait to pay for something by using a credit card

charge card: a plastic card used to put off paying for something

checkout: the place in a store where you pay for the items you want to buy

clerk: a person who works in a store

credit card: a plastic card used to pay for items. Later, a bill is sent, telling you how much money is owed

debt: money that you owe to someone else

dread: being very afraid of something

jeer: to speak loudly to someone in a mean way

plastic: a nickname for a credit card

About the Author

In fifth grade English class, Mary (Leary) Becker discovered her love of writing; that was the same year she discovered how fun it can be to spend money! Many years and purchases later, those two interests now combine in the entertaining and educational story of the I. O. Lots family. The author's hope is that *The Debt Monster* will lead families to great discussions about how to be wise stewards with their finances. Mary is presently living happily-ever-after with her high school sweetheart/husband in a storybook cottage, which includes a revolving door that is always open to their seven children, their children's spouses, and grandchildren.

For more information or other books by

Mary Becker,

please visit

MaryBeckerBooks.com

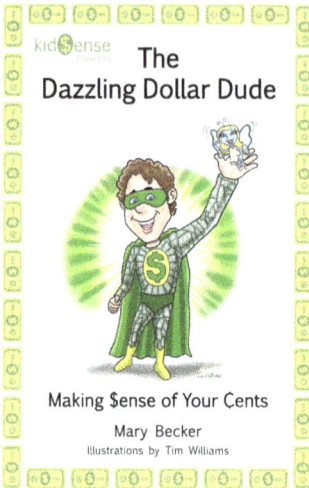

The
Dazzling Dollar Dude

Making $ense of Your Cents

Mary Becker
Illustrations by Tim Williams

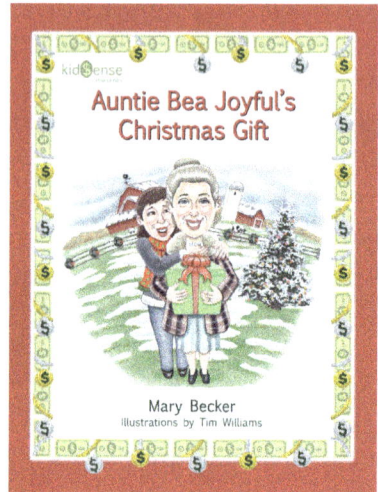

Auntie Bea Joyful's
Christmas Gift

Mary Becker
Illustrations by Tim Williams

You can also follow us on

Mary Becker Author

Thank you for reading my book.
Please consider sharing it with friends or family
and leaving a review online. Your feedback and
support are very much appreciated.

www.ingramcontent.com/pod-product-compliance
Lightning Source LLC
Chambersburg PA
CBHW071532210326
41597CB00018B/2970